Love Letters of
GREAT MEN

*From Beethoven to Bonaparte
and Beyond*

The Collection of Love Letters
Drawn from by Carrie Bradshaw in
"Sex in the City"

By

Ludwig Van Beethoven, François-Marie Arouet
Voltaire, John Adams, Vincent Van Gogh,
Dylan Thomas, Wolfgang Amadeus Mozart

Love Letters of Great Men

Published by
ReadaClassic.com

ISBN#: 978-1-44216-385-0

Table of Contents

Adams, John
Second President of the United States

Adams, John

John Adams (1735-1826) and Abigail Smith Adams (1744-1818) exchanged over 1,100 letters, beginning during their courtship in 1762 and continuing throughout John's political career. These warm and informative letters include John's descriptions of the Continental Congress and his impressions of Europe while he served in various diplomatic roles, as well as Abigail's updates about their family, farm, and news of the Revolution's impact on the Boston area. John Adams was an American politician and political philosopher who served as the first Vice President of the United States and second President of the United States. He was one of the most influential Founding Fathers of the U.S.

Adams came to prominence in the early stages of the American Revolution. As a delegate from Massachusetts to the Continental Congress, he played a leading role in persuading Congress to declare independence, and assisted Thomas Jefferson in drafting the United States Declaration of Independence in 1776. As a representative of Congress in Europe, he was a major negotiator of the eventual peace treaty with Great Britain, and chiefly responsible for obtaining important loans from Amsterdam bankers.

After Adams was defeated for reelection by Thomas Jefferson (at the time, Adams' vice-president), he retired to Massachusetts. He and Abigail were the progenitors of an accomplished family line of politicians, diplomats, and historians now referred to as the "Adams political family." One of their most well-known descendants was John Quincy Adams, the sixth President of the United States.

Although the elder John Adams achievements were not initially as celebrated as those of the other founders, they have received greater recognition in modern times.

My dearest Friend

I have written three answers to yours of January 4. This is the fourth. The three first I have burned. In one I was melancholy, in another angry, and in the third merry—but either would have given you more pain than pleasure. I have gone through with several others of your letters in the same manner. They are admirably written, but there is such a strain of unhappiness and complaint in them, as has made me very uneasy.

This last goes farther than any other, and contains an expression which alarms me indeed, and convinces me, either that some infernal has whispered in your ear insinuations, or that you have forgotten the unalterable tenderness of my heart.

This letter is an additional motive with me to come home. It is time. I have written as often as I could. I want to write you every day but I cannot—I have too much to say: but have good reasons for saying nothing. Is it necessary that I should make protestations that I am, with an heart as pure as gold or ether.*

Forever yours.

John Adams

Early meanings of the word ether include the clear sky, the upper regions of space beyond the clouds, or the element breathed by the gods.

Ballou, Sullivan
Lawyer and Civil War Soldier

Ballou, Sullivan

Sullivan Ballou (1829–1861) was a lawyer, politician, and major in the United States Army. He is best remembered for the eloquent letter he wrote to his wife a week before he fought and was mortally wounded alongside his Rhode Island Volunteers in the First Battle of Bull Run.

When war broke out, Ballou immediately left what appeared to be a promising political career and volunteered for military service with the 2nd Rhode Island Infantry. In addition to his combat duties, he served as the Rhode Island militia's judge advocate.

Ballou and 93 of his men were mortally wounded at Bull Run. In an attempt to better direct his men, Ballou took a horse mounted position in front of his regiment, when a 6-pounder solid shot from Confederate artillery tore off his right leg and simultaneously killed his horse. The badly injured Major was then carried off the field and the remainder of his leg was amputated. Ballou died from his wound a week after that Union defeat and was buried in the yard of nearby Sudley Church.

Ballou had married Sarah Hunt Shumway on October 15, 1855. They had two sons, Edgar and William. In his letter to Sarah, Ballou attempted to crystallize the emotions he was feeling: worry, fear, guilt, sadness and, most importantly, the pull between his love for her and his sense of duty. While not a famous man in the sense of the others featured in this book, Sullivan was great in his concern for his family and willingness to lay down his life for his country. The following is an excerpt of his letter.

July the 14th, 1861
Washington D.C.

My very dear Sarah:

The indications are very strong that we shall move in a few days—perhaps tomorrow. Lest I should not be able to write you again, I feel impelled to write lines that may fall under your eye when I shall be no more.

Our movement may be one of a few days duration and full of pleasure—and it may be one of severe conflict and death to me. Not my will, but thine O God, be done. If it is necessary that I should fall on the battlefield for my country, I am ready. I have no misgivings about, or lack of confidence in, the cause in which I am engaged, and my courage does not halt or falter. I know how strongly American Civilization now leans upon the triumph of the Government, and how great a debt we owe to those who went before us through the blood and suffering of the Revolution. And I am willing—perfectly willing—to lay down all my joys in this life, to help maintain this Government, and to pay that debt.

But, my dear wife, when I know that with my own joys I lay down nearly all of yours, and replace them in this life with cares and sorrows—when, after having eaten for long years the bitter fruit of orphanage myself, I must offer it as their only sustenance to my dear little children—is it weak or dishonorable, while the banner of my purpose floats calmly and proudly in the breeze, that my unbounded love for you, my darling wife and children, should struggle in fierce, though useless, contest with my love of country?

Love Letters of Great Men

I cannot describe to you my feelings on this calm summer night, when two thousand men are sleeping around me, many of them enjoying the last, perhaps, before that of death—and I, suspicious that Death is creeping behind me with his fatal dart, am communing with God, my country, and thee.

I have sought most closely and diligently, and often in my breast, for a wrong motive in thus hazarding the happiness of those I loved and I could not find one. A pure love of my country and of the principles have often advocated before the people and "the name of honor that I love more than I fear death" have called upon me, and I have obeyed.

Sarah, my love for you is deathless, it seems to bind me to you with mighty cables that nothing but Omnipotence could break; and yet my love of Country comes over me like a strong wind and bears me irresistibly on with all these chains to the battlefield.

The memories of the blissful moments I have spent with you come creeping over me, and I feel most gratified to God and to you that I have enjoyed them so long. And hard it is for me to give them up and burn to ashes the hopes of future years, when God willing, we might still have lived and loved together and seen our sons grow up to honorable manhood around us. I have, I know, but few and small claims upon Divine Providence, but something whispers to me—perhaps it is the wafted prayer of my little Edgar—that I shall return to my loved ones unharmed.

If I do not, my dear Sarah, never forget how much I love you, and when my last breath escapes me on the battlefield, it will whisper your name.

Forgive my many faults, and the many pains I have caused you. How thoughtless and foolish I have oftentimes been! How gladly would I wash out with my tears every little spot upon your happiness, and struggle with all the misfortune of this world, to shield you and my children from harm. But I cannot... Sarah, do not mourn me dead; think I am gone and wait for thee, for we shall meet again.

As for my little boys, they will grow as I have done, and never know a father's love and care. Little Willie is too young to remember me long, and my blue-eyed Edgar will keep my frolics with him among the dimmest memories of his childhood. Sarah, I have unlimited confidence in your maternal care and your development of their characters. Tell my two mothers his and hers I call God's blessing upon them. O Sarah, I wait for you there! Come to me, and lead thither my children.

Sullivan

Balzac, Honoré de
French Novelist and Playwright

Balzac, Honoré de

Honoré de Balzac (1799–1850) was a French novelist and playwright. His magnum opus was a sequence of almost 100 novels, short stories and plays collectively entitled La Comédie Humaine, which presents a panorama of French life in the years after the fall of Napoléon Bonaparte in 1815. Due to his keen observation of detail and unfiltered representation of society, Balzac is regarded as one of the founders of realism in European literature. He is renowned for his multi-faceted characters; even his lesser characters are complex, morally ambiguous and fully human. Inanimate objects are imbued with character as well; the city of Paris, a backdrop for much of his writing, takes on many human qualities.

An enthusiastic reader and independent thinker as a child, Balzac had trouble adapting to the teaching style of his grammar school. His willful nature caused trouble throughout his life, and frustrated his ambitions to succeed in the world of business. When he finished school, Balzac was apprenticed as a legal clerk, but turned his back on law after wearying of its inhumanity and banal routine. Before and during his career as a writer, he attempted to be a publisher, printer, businessman, critic, and politician. He failed in all of these efforts. La Comédie Humaine reflects his real-life difficulties, and includes scenes from his own experience.

Balzac suffered from health problems throughout his life, possibly due to his intense writing schedule. His relationship with his family was often strained by financial and personal drama, and he lost more than one friend over critical reviews. In 1850 he married Evelina Hańska, his longtime love; he died five months later.

Love Letters of Great Men

June, 1836
My beloved angel,

I am nearly mad about you, as much as one can be mad: I cannot bring together two ideas that you do not interpose yourself between them.

I can no longer think of anything but you. In spite of myself, my imagination carries me to you. I grasp you, I kiss you, I caress you, a thousand of the most amorous caresses take possession of me.

As for my heart, there you will always be—very much so. I have a delicious sense of you there. But my God, what is to become of me, if you have deprived me of my reason? This is a monomania which, this morning, terrifies me.

I rise up every moment saying to myself, "Come, I am going there!" Then I sit down again, moved by the sense of my obligations. There is a frightful conflict. This is not life. I have never before been like that. You have devoured everything.

I feel foolish and happy as soon as I think of you. I whirl round in a delicious dream in which in one instant I live a thousand years. What a horrible situation!

Overcome with love, feeling love in every pore, living only for love, and seeing oneself consumed by griefs, and caught in a thousand spiders' threads.

O, my darling Eva, you did not know it. I picked up your card. It is there before me, and I talk to you as if you were there. I see you, as I did yesterday, beautiful, astonishingly beautiful. Yesterday, during the whole evening, I said to myself "she is mine!" Ah! The angels are not as happy in Paradise as I was yesterday!

Honoré de Balzac
To Evelina Hanska, the Polish countess who he later married

Beethoven, Ludwig van
Famous and influential German composer

Beethoven, Ludwig van

Ludwig van Beethoven (1770-1827), one of history's most famous and mysterious composers died at the age of 57 with one great secret. These letters were found in Beethoven's desk after he died. They were not addressed to anybody, so it is impossible to know who he was writing to. It was written to an unknown woman who Beethoven simply called his "Immortal Beloved."

The world may never put a face with this mysterious woman or know the circumstances of their affair, and his letters are all that is left of a love as intensely passionate as the music for which Beethoven became famous. Compositions such as the Moonlight Sonata as well as Beethoven's many symphonies express eloquently the tragedy of a relationship never publicly realized.

July 6, in the morning

My angel, my all, my very self—Only a few words today and at that with pencil (with yours)—Not till tomorrow will my lodgings be definitely determined upon—what a useless waste of time—Why this deep sorrow when necessity speaks—can our love endure except through sacrifices, through not demanding everything from one another; can you change the fact that you are not wholly mine, I not wholly thine—Oh God, look out into the beauties of nature and comfort your heart with that which must be—Love demands everything and that very justly—thus it is to me with you, and to your with me.

But you forget so easily that I must live for me and for you; if we were wholly united you would feel the pain of it as little as I—My journey was a fearful one; I did not reach here until 4 o'clock yesterday morning. Lacking horses the post-coach chose another route, but what an awful one; at the stage before the last I was warned not to travel at night; I was made fearful of a forest, but that only made me the more eager—and I was wrong.

The coach must needs break down on the wretched road, a bottomless mud road. Without such postilions as I had with me I should have remained stuck in the road. Esterhazy, traveling the usual road here, had the same fate with eight horses that I had with four—Yet I got some pleasure out of it, as I always do when I successfully overcome difficulties—Now a quick change to things internal from things external. We shall surely see each other soon; moreover, today I cannot share with you the thoughts I have had during these last few days touching my

20

own life—If our hearts were always close together, I would have none of these. My heart is full of so many things to say to you—ah—there are moments when I feel that speech amounts to nothing at all—Cheer up—remain my true, my only treasure, my all as I am yours. The gods must send us the rest, what for us must and shall be—

Your faithful Ludwig

Good morning, on July 7

Though still in bed, my thoughts go out to you, my Immortal Beloved, now and then joyfully, then sadly, waiting to learn whether or not fate will hear us—I can live only wholly with you or not at all—Yes, I am resolved to wander so long away from you until I can fly to your arms and say that I am really at home with you, and can send my soul enwrapped in you into the land of spirits—Yes, unhappily it must be so—You will be the more contained since you know my fidelity to you. No one else can ever possess my heart—never—never—Oh God, why must one be parted from one whom one so loves. And yet my life in V is now a wretched life—Your love makes me at once the happiest and the unhappiest of men—At my age I need a steady, quiet life—can that be so in our connection? My angel, I have just been told that the mailcoach goes every day— therefore I must close at once so that you may receive the letter at once—Be calm, only by a calm consideration of our existence can we achieve our purpose to live together—Be calm—love me—today—yesterday—what tearful longings for you—you—you—my life—my all—farewell. Oh continue to love me—never misjudge the most faithful heart of your beloved.

ever thine
ever mine
ever ours*

*The letter above,by Ludwig Van Beethoven, is the letter Mr. Big quotes at the wedding with Carrie in "Sex and the City."

Bonaparte, Napoleon
Famous French Military Commander

Bonaparte, Napoleon

Napoleon Bonaparte (1769-1821) was born in Corsica. He became an army officer in 1785, and after rapid promotion, took command of the army of the interior in 1795. After a coup in 1799, Napoleon became first consul, and in 1804 emperor. Between 1804 and 1810 he consolidated his empire in Europe.

In 1814, following defeat in Russia, he abdicated and was banished to Elba. In 1815 he resumed power, but was crushed at the Battle of Waterloo and exiled to St. Helena, where he died in 1821.

In addition to being a brilliant military mind and feared ruler, Napolean Bonaparte was a prolific writer of letters. He reportedly wrote as many as 75,000 letters in his lifetime, many of them to his beautiful wife, Josephine, both before and during their marriage. This letter, written just prior to their 1796 wedding, shows surprising tenderness and emotion from the future emperor.

Paris
December 1795

I wake filled with thoughts of you. Your portrait and the intoxicating evening which we spent yesterday have left my senses in turmoil. Sweet, incomparable Josephine, what a strange effect you have on my heart! Are you angry? Do I see you looking sad? Are you worried?... My soul aches with sorrow, and there can be no rest for your lover; but is there still more in store for me when, yielding to the profound feelings which overwhelm me, I draw from your lips, from your heart a love which consumes me with fire? Ah! it was last night that I fully realized how false an image of you your portrait gives!

You are leaving at noon; I shall see you in three hours.

Until then, mio dolce amor, a thousand kisses; but give me none in return, for they set my blood on fire.

Spring 1797

To Josephine,

I love you no longer; on the contrary, I detest you. you are a wretch, truly perverse, truly stupid, a real Cinderella. You never write to me at all, you do not love your husband; you know the pleasure that your letters give him yet you cannot even manage to write him half a dozen lines, dashed off in a moment! What then do you do all day, Madame? What business is so vital that it robs you of the time to write to your faithful lover? What attachment can be stifling and pushing aside the love, the tender and constant love which you promised him? Who can this wonderful new lover be who takes up your every moment, rules your days and prevents you from devoting your attention to your husband?

Beware, Josephine; one fine night the doors will be broken down and there I shall be. In truth, I am worried, my love, to have no news from you; write me a four page letter instantly made up from those delightful words which fill my heart with emotion and joy. I hope to hold you in my arms before long, when I shall lavish upon you a million kisses, burning as the equatorial sun.

Browning, Robert

English poet and playwright whose mastery of dramatic verse
made him one of the foremost Victorian poets

Browning, Robert

Robert Browning (1812–889) was an English poet and playwright whose mastery of dramatic verse, especially dramatic monologues, made him one of the foremost Victorian poets.

The courtship and marriage between Robert Browning and Elizabeth Barrett was carried out secretly. Six years his elder and an invalid, Elizabeth could not believe that the vigorous and worldly Browning really loved her as much as he professed to, and her doubts are expressed in the Sonnets from the Portuguese, which she wrote over the next two years. Love conquered all, however, and, after a private marriage at St Marylebone Parish Church, Browning imitated his hero Shelley by spiriting his beloved off to Italy in August 1846, which became her home almost continuously until her death. Elizabeth's loyal nurse, Wilson, who witnessed the marriage at the church, accompanied the couple to Italy and became at service to them.

After her marriage to Robert Browning, Elizabeth's father disinherited her (as he did for each of his children who married). "The Mrs. Browning of popular imagination was a sweet, innocent young woman who suffered endless cruelties at the hands of a tyrannical papa but who nonetheless had the good fortune to fall in love with a dashing and handsome poet named Robert Browning. She finally escaped the dungeon of Wimpole Street, eloped to Italy, and lived happily ever after."

January 10th, 1845
New Cross, Hatcham, Surrey

I love your verses with all my heart, dear Miss Barrett,—and this is no off-hand complimentary letter that I shall write,—whatever else, no prompt matter-of-course recognition of your genius and there a graceful and natural end of the thing: since the day last week when I first read your poems, I quite laugh to remember how I have been turning again in my mind what I should be able to tell you of their effect upon me—for in the first flush of delight I thought I would this once get out of my habit of purely passive enjoyment, when I do really enjoy, and thoroughly justify my admiration—perhaps even, as a loyal fellow-craftsman should, try and find fault and do you some little good to be proud of herafter! —but nothing comes of it all—so into me has it gone, and part of me has it become, this great living poetry of yours, not a flower of which but took root and grew...

Oh, how different that is from lying to be dried and pressed flat and prized highly and put in a book with a proper account at bottom, and shut up and put away ... and the book called a 'Flora', besides! After all, I need not give up the thought of doing that, too, in time; because even now, talking with whoever is worthy, I can give reason for my faith in one and another excellence, the fresh strange music, the affluent language, the exquisite pathos and true new brave thought—but in this addressing myself to you, your own self, and for the first time, my feeling rises altogher.

I do, as I say, love these Books with all my heart—and I love you too: do you know I was once seeing you? Mr. Kenyon said to me one morning "would you like to see Miss Barrett?"—

then he went to announce me,—then he returned...you were too unwell—and now it is years ago—and I feel as at some untorward passage in my travels—as if I had been close, so close, to some world's-wonder in chapel on crypt...only a screen to push and I might have entered—but there was some slight ...so it now seems...slight and just-sufficient bar to admission, and the half-opened door shut, and I went home my thousands of miles, and the sight was never to be!

Well, these Poems were to be—and this true thankful joy and pride with which I feel myself.

Yours ever faithfully
Robert Browning

Burns, Robert

Scottish poet and lyricist, widely regarded as the
national poet of Scotland

Burns, Robert

Robert Burns (1759–1796), a Scottish poet and lyricist, is known as Scotland's favorite son and the Ploughman Poet. He is also widely regarded as the national poet of Scotland, and is celebrated worldwide. The best known of the poets who have written in the Scots language, Burns also wrote many of his poems in English with a "light" Scots dialect. He also wrote in standard English, and in these pieces, his political or civil commentary is often at its most blunt.

He is regarded as a pioneer of the Romantic movement and after his death became a great source of inspiration to the founders of both liberalism and socialism. A cultural icon in Scotland and among the Scottish Diaspora around the world, celebration of his life and work became almost a national charismatic cult during the 19th and 20th centuries, and his influence has long been strong on Scottish literature. In 2009 he was voted by the Scottish public as being the Greatest Scot, through a vote run by Scottish television channel STV.

Burns wrote a tremendous number of love letters during his relatively short but very full life. Known for his many affairs, Burns was adept at using his writing ability to appeal to the heart of the women to whom he wrote his love letters and romantic poetry. The following letter was written to someone with whom he is not yet having an affair—but was hoping to do so.

Dear Madam,

The passion of love has need to be productive of much delight; as where it takes thorough possession of the man, it almost unfits him for anything else.

The lover who is certain of an equal return of affection, is surely the happiest of men; but he who is a prey to the horrors of anxiety and dreaded disappointment, is a being whose situation is by no means enviable.

Of this, my present experience gives me much proof.

To me, amusement seems impertinent, and business intrusion, while you alone engross every faculty of my mind.

May I request you to drop me a line, to inform me when I may wait upon you?

For pity's sake, do; and let me have it soon.

In the meantime allow me, in all the artless sincerity of truth, to assure you that I truly am, my dearest Madam, your ardent lover, and devoted humble servant.

Byron, Lord
Famous British poet and a leading figure in the Romantic movement

Byron, Lord

Lord Byron, was a British poet and a leading figure in Romanticism. He is regarded as one of the greatest British poets and remains widely read and influential, both in the English-speaking world and beyond.

Byron's notability rests not only on his writings but also on his life, which featured aristocratic excesses, huge debts, numerous love affairs, and self-imposed exile. Byron served as a regional leader of Italy's revolutionary organisation, the Carbonari, in its struggle against Austria. He later travelled to fight against the Ottoman Empire in the Greek War of Independence, for which Greeks revere him as a national hero.

In 1812, Byron embarked on a well-publicised affair with the married Lady Caroline Lamb that shocked the British public. Byron eventually broke off the relationship and moved swiftly on to others (such as that with Lady Oxford), but Lamb never entirely recovered, pursuing him even after he tired of her. She was emotionally disturbed, and lost so much weight that Byron cruelly commented to her mother-in-law, his friend Lady Melbourne, that he was "haunted by a skeleton". She began to call on him at home, sometimes dressed in disguise as a page boy, at a time when such an act could ruin both of them socially. One day, during such a visit, she wrote on a book at his desk, "Remember me!" As a retort, Byron wrote a poem entitled Remember Thee! Remember Thee! which concludes with the line "Thou false to him, thou fiend to me".

As for Lady Caroline Lamb, she famously described Lord Byron as "mad, bad and dangerous to know".

Love Letters of Great Men

Lord Byron to Lady Caroline Lamb
August 1812

My dearest Caroline,

If tears, which you saw & know I am not apt to shed, if the agitation in which I parted from you, agitation which you must have perceived through the whole of this most nervous nervous affair, did not commence till the moment of leaving you approached, if all that I have said & done, & am still but too ready to say & do, have not sufficiently proved what my real feelings are & must be ever towards you, my love, I have no other proof to offer.

God knows I wish you happy, & when I quit you, or rather when you from a sense of duty to your husband & mother quit me, you shall acknowledge the truth of what I again promise & vow, that no other in word or deed shall ever hold the place in my affection which is & shall be most sacred to you, till I am nothing.

I never knew till that moment, the madness of—my dearest & most beloved friend—I cannot express myself—this is no time for words -- but I shall have a pride, a melancholy pleasure, in suffering what you yourself can hardly conceive—for you do not know me.—I am now about to go out with a heavy heart, because—my appearing this Evening will stop any absurd story which the events of today might give rise to—do you think now that I am cold & stern, & artful—will even others think so, will your mother even—that mother to whom we must indeed sacrifice much, more much more on my part, than she shall ever know or can imagine.

"Promises not to love you" ah Caroline it is past promising—but shall attribute all concessions to the proper motive—& never cease to feel all that you have already witnessed—& more than can ever be known but to my own heart—perhaps to yours—May God protect forgive & bless you—ever & even more than ever.

Yr. most attached
BYRON

P.S.—These taunts which have driven you to this—my dearest Caroline—were it not for your mother & the kindness of all your connections, is there anything on earth or heaven would have made me so happy as to have made you mine long ago? & not less now than then, but more than ever at this time—you know I would with pleasure give up all here & all beyond the grave for you—& in refraining from this —must my motives be misunderstood—? I care not who knows this—what use is made of it—it is you & to you only that they owe yourself, I was and am yours, freely & most entirely, to obey, to honour, love—& fly with you when, where, & how you yourself might & may determine.

Churchill, Winston
Prime Minister of the United Kingdom during World War II

Churchill, Winston

Winston Churchill's marriage to Clementine Hozier was a lasting and happy one but they also had fiery arguments. Clementine was a determined, dignified, loyal, sympathetic and yet also challenging partner. She was the critic Winston heeded above all others.

During their fifty-six year marriage, Winston and Clementine wrote warmly to one another whenever they were apart. They even wrote love notes back and forth to each other while living in the same house. Their letters and notes often ended with drawings illustrating their pet names for each other. He was her "pug" (a breed of dog) and she was his "cat."

Churchill's letter to his wife Clementine really sums up the mature love which succeeds romantic love and passion in a long marriage.

January 23, 1935
My darling Clemmie,

In your letter from Madras you wrote some words very dear to me, about my having enriched your life. I cannot tell you what pleasure this gave me, because I always feel so overwhelmingly in your debt, if there can be accounts in love.... What it has been to me to live all these years in your heart and companionship no phrases can convey.

Time passes swiftly, but is it not joyous to see how great and growing is the treasure we have gathered together, amid the storms and stresses of so many eventful and to millions tragic and terrible years?

Your loving husband

(Winston Churchill)

Curie, Pierre
French Physicist and Nobel Laureate

Curie, Pierre

Pierre Curie (1859–1906) was a French physicist, a pioneer in crystallography, magnetism, piezoelectricity and radioactivity, and Nobel laureate. In 1903 he received the Nobel Prize in Physics with his wife, Maria Skłodowska-Curie (Madame Curie), and Henri Becquerel, "in recognition of the extraordinary services they have rendered by their joint researches on the radiation phenomena discovered by Professor Henri Becquerel".

Pierre and Marie Curie's daughter Irène Joliot-Curie and their son-in-law Frédéric Joliot-Curie were also physicists involved in the study of radioactivity. They also were awarded a Nobel prize for their work.

The Curies' other daughter, Ève, wrote a noted biography of her mother.

In April 1995 Pierre and Marie Curie were enshrined in the crypt of the Panthéon in Paris.

August 10, 1894

Nothing could have given me greater pleasure that to get news of you. The prospect of remaining two months without hearing about you had been extremely disagreeable to me: that is to say, your little note was more than welcome.

I hope you are laying up a stock of good air and that you will come back to us in October. As for me, I think I shall not go anywhere; I shall stay in the country, where I spend the whole day in front of my open window or in the garden.

We have promised each other—haven't we?—to be at least great friends. If you will only not change your mind! For there are no promises that are binding; such things cannot be ordered at will. It would be a fine thing, just the same, in which I hardly dare believe, to pass our lives near each other, hypnotized by our dreams: your patriotic dream, our humanitarian dream, and our scientific dream.

Of all those dreams the last is, I believe, the only legitimate one. I mean by that that we are powerless to change the social order and, even if we were not, we should not know what to do; in taking action, no matter in what direction, we should never be sure of not doing more harm than good, by retarding some inevitable evolution. From the scientific point of view, on the contrary, we may hope to do something; the ground is solider here, and any discovery that we may make, however small, will remain acquired knowledge.

See how it works out: it is agreed that we shall be great friends, but if you leave France in a year it would be an altogether too Platonic friendship, that of two creatures who would never see each other again. Wouldn't it be better for you to stay with me? I know that this question angers you, and that you don't want to speak of it again—and then, too, I feel so thoroughly unworthy of you from every point of view.

Pierre

Marie Curie

I thought of asking your permission to meet you by chance in Fribourg. But you are staying there, unless I am   mistaken, only one day, and on that day you will of course belong to our friends the Kovalskis.

Believe me your very devoted
Pierre Curie

Fitzgerald, F. Scott

American novelist and short story writer

Fitzgerald, F. Scott

One hot Alabama night in July 1918, 23-year-old Francis Scott Fitzgerald, an infantry officer and aspiring writer, met young Zelda Sayre at a Country Club dance in her hometown, Montgomery. She was a teenage whirlwind, just out of high school, sweeping up the beaus of the town—the "jellybeans" as they were known--in her wake. Several weeks later Scott seemed to have made up his mind to marry Zelda. A diary entry for September 1918 reads:

"Fell in love on the 7th."
Zelda Sayre to F. Scott Fitzgerald

Zelda, the daughter of an Alabama High Court judge, was intelligent and strikingly beautiful, but also wild. The Fitzgeralds married in 1920, but after several years of high and happy living (financed by Scott's success as a writer and shaped by his drinking), Zelda's behavior became erratic and obsessive, and their relationship more strained.

F. Scott Fitzgerald, who was born in St. Paul, Minnesota, gained instant fame with his first novel This Side of Paradise. Together with Zelda, he came to represent the "Jazz Age", both in his writing and in lifestyle, with his wildness, generosity, heavy drinking, partying, and high spending. His finest novel was The Great Gatsby, the story of rich financier Jay gatsby's disastrous love for Daisy Buchanan and a key exploration of "The American Dream". Fitzgerald's final novel, The Last Tycoon, was unfinished when he died.

Love Letters of Great Men

Letter from Zelda to Scott
Spring 1919

Sweetheart,

Please, please don't be so depressed—We'll be married soon,
and then these lonesome nights will be over forever—and until
we are, I am loving, loving every tiny minute of the day and
night—Maybe you won't understand this, but sometimes when
I miss you most, it's hardest to write—and you always know
when I make myself—Just the ache of it all—and I can't tell
you. If we were together, you'd feel how strong it is—you're so
sweet when you're melancholy. I love your sad tenderness—
when I've hurt you—That's one of the reasons I could never be
sorry for our quarrels—and they bothered you so—Those dear,
dear little fusses, when I always tried so hard to make you kiss
and forget—

Scott—there's nothing in all the world I want but you—and
your precious love—All the materials things are nothing. I'd
just hate to live a sordid, colorless existence—because you'd
soon love me less—and less—and I'd do anything—
anything—to keep your heart for my own—I don't want to
live—I want to love first, and live incidentally...Don't—don't
ever think of the things you can't give me—You've trusted me
with the dearest heart of all—and it's so damn much more than
anybody else in all the world has ever had—

How can you think deliberately of life without me—If you
should die—O Darling—darling Scott—It'd be like going
blind...I'd have no purpose in life—just a pretty—decoration.
Don't you think I was made for you? I feel like you had me

ordered—and I was delivered to you—to be worn—I want you to wear me, like a watch—charm or a button hole bouquet—to the world. And then, when we're alone, I want to help—to know that you can't do anything without me...

All my heart—
I love you

Hawthorne, Nathaniel
American novelist and short story writer

Hawthorne, Nathaniel

Nathaniel Hawthorne (1804 - 1864) was forty-six years old before he obtained his first literary success. Hawthorne would repeatedly credit his wife, Sophia, as his muse. Shy and reclusive, Hawthorne first met Sophia Peabody in 1838, when he was still a struggling and largely unimpressive writer. In this letter, the newly married Hawthorne struggles to find the proper words of love to offer his wife.

The Hawthornes enjoyed a long marriage, often taking walks in the park. Of his wife, whom he referred to as his "Dove", Hawthorne wrote that she "is, in the strictest sense, my sole companion; and I need no other—there is no vacancy in my mind, any more than in my heart... Thank God that I suffice for her boundless heart!" Sophia greatly admired her husband's work. In one of her journals, she wrote: "I am always so dazzled and bewildered with the richness, the depth, the...jewels of beauty in his productions that I am always looking forward to a second reading where I can ponder and muse and fully take in the miraculous wealth of thoughts".

5 December, 1839

Dearest,—I wish I had the gift of making rhymes, for methinks there is poetry in my head and heart since I have been in love with you. You are a Poem. Of what sort, then? Epic? Mercy on me, no! A sonnet? No; for that is too labored and artificial. You are a sort of sweet, simple, gay, pathetic ballad, which Nature is singing, sometimes with tears, sometimes with smiles, and sometimes with intermingled smiles and tears.

Henry VI of France

French monarch who showed great care for his subjects and
unusual religious tolerance for his time

Henry VI of France

Henry IV (1553–1610) was King of France from 1589 to 1610 and (as Henry III) King of Navarre from 1572 to 1610. He was the first monarch of the Bourbon branch of the Capetian dynasty in France.

Gabrielle d'Estrées became Henry's mistress in 1591. Although Henry IV was married to Marguerite de Valois, Henri and Gabrielle were openly affectionate with each other in public. Fiercely loyal, Gabrielle accompanied Henri during his campaigns. Even when heavily pregnant, she insisted on living inside his tent near the battlefield, making sure his clothing was clean and that he ate well after a battle, handling the correspondence while he fought.

The relationship between Henri and Gabrielle did not sit well with some members of the French aristocracy, and malicious pamphlets circulated that blamed the new duchess for many national misfortunes. One of the most vicious nicknames ascribed to Gabrielle was la duchesse d'Ordure ("the Duchess of Filth").

After applying to Pope Clement VIII for an annulment of his marriage and authority to marry Gabrielle, in March of 1599 Henri gave his mistress his coronation ring. Gabrielle, so sure that the wedding would take place, stated, "Only God or the king's death could put an end to my good luck". A few days later, on 9 April, she suffered an attack of eclampsia and gave birth to a stillborn son.

King Henri was at the Château de Fontainebleau when news arrived of her illness. The next day, 10 April 1599, while Henri was on his way to her, she died in Paris after the miscarriage.

The king was grief-stricken, especially given the widely-held rumor that Gabrielle had been poisoned. He wore black in mourning, something no previous French monarch had done before.

Love Letters of Great Men

Letter to Gabrielle d'Estrées
From the battle field before Dreux

June 16, 1593

I have waited patiently for one whole day without news of you;
I have been counting the time and that's what it must be. But a
second day—I can see no reason for it, unless my servants have
grown lazy or been captured by the enemy, for I dare not put
the blame on you, my beautiful angel: I am too confident of
your affection—which is certainly due to me, for my love was
never greater, nor my desire more urgent; that is why I repeat
this refrain in all my letters: come, come, come, my dear love.
Honor with your presence the man who, if only he were free,
would go a thousand miles to throw himself at your feet and
never move from there. As for what is happening here, we have
drained the water from the moat, but our cannons are not going
to be in place until Friday when, God willing, I will dine in
town.

The day after you reach Mantes, my sister will arrive at Anet,
where I will have the pleasure of seeing you every day. I am
sending you a bouquet of orange blossom that I have just
received. I kiss the hands of the Vicomtess if she is there, and
of my good friend, and as for you, my dear love, I kiss your
feet a million times.

Hugo, Victor

French poet, playwright, novelist, and essayist

Hugo, Victor

Victor-Marie Hugo (1802-85) was born in France, the third son of an army general. A sickly infant, he was not expected to live, but grew more robust from the age of two when he went to live with his mother in Paris—"the birthplace of my soul."

As a teenager, Hugo began to fill notebooks with poetry. In maturity he was a prolific and very successful poet, dramatist, and novelist, and the most celebrated author of his generation.

For three years Victor Hugo and Adele Foucher exchanged secret messages. The following letter was written shortly after Hugo was promised a pension from Louis XVIII as a reward for his loyalty. This pension allowed the couple to marry. Their marriage lasted until Adele's death in 1868.

Friday evening, March 15, 1822.

After the two delightful evenings spent yesterday and the day before, I shall certainly not go out tonight, but will sit here at home and write to you. Besides, my Adele, my adorable and adored Adele, what have I not to tell you? O, God! for two days, I have been asking myself every moment if such happiness is not a dream. It seems to me that what I feel is not of earth. I cannot yet comprehend this cloudless heaven.

You do not yet know, Adele, to what I had resigned myself. Alas, do I know it myself? Because I was weak, I fancied I was calm; because I was preparing myself for all the mad follies of despair, I thought I was courageous and resigned. Ah! let me cast myself humbly at your feet, you who are so grand, so tender and strong! I had been thinking that the utmost limit of my devotion could only be the sacrifice of my life; but you, my generous love, were ready to sacrifice for me the repose of yours.

...You have been privileged to receive every gift from nature, you have both fortitude and tears. Oh, Adele, do not mistake these words for blind enthusiasm - enthusiasm for you has lasted all my life, and increased day by day. My whole soul is yours. If my entire existence had not been yours, the harmony of my being would have been lost, and I must have died — died inevitably.

These were my meditations, Adele, when the letter that was to bring me hope of else despair arrived. If you love me, you know what must have been my joy. What I know you may have felt, I will not describe.

My Adele, why is there no word for this but joy? Is it because there is no power in human speech to express such happiness? The sudden bound from mournful resignation to infinite felicity seemed to upset me. Even now I am still beside myself and sometimes I tremble lest I should suddenly awaken from this dream divine.

Oh, now you are mine! At last you are mine! Soon — in a few months, perhaps, my angel will sleep in my arms, will awaken in my arms, will live there. All your thoughts at all moments, all your looks will be for me; all my thoughts, all my moments, all my looks, will be for you! My Adele!

Adieu, my angel, my beloved Adele! Adieu! I will kiss your hair and go to bed. Still I am far from you, but I can dream of you. Soon perhaps you will be at my side. Adieu; pardon the delirium of your husband who embraces you, and who adores you, both for this life and another.

Joyce, James

Influential Irish poet and novelist

Joyce, James

James Joyce (1882–1941) was an Irish writer and poet, widely considered to be one of the most influential writers of the 20th century. Along with Marcel Proust, Virginia Woolf, and others, Joyce was a key figure in the development of the modernist novel. He is best known for his landmark novel Ulysses. Other major works are the short-story collection Dubliners, and the novels A Portrait of the Artist as a Young Man and Finnegans Wake.

While on his first return trip to Dublin from Zurich in 1909, James Joyce wrote a series of romantic (and quite erotic) letters to his long-time girlfriend (and future wife) Nora Barnacle. In the words of Nora herself, "I don't know whether my husband is a genius or not, but he certainly has a dirty mind." This letter is no doubt one of the tamest of the bunch...

Love Letter from James Joyce to Nora Barnacle
(August 15, 1904)

My dear Nora,

It has just struck me. I came in at half past eleven. Since then I have been sitting in an easy chair like a fool. I could do nothing. I hear nothing but your voice. I am like a fool hearing you call me 'Dear.' I offended two men today by leaving them coolly. I wanted to hear your voice, not theirs.

When I am with you I leave aside my contemptuous, suspicious nature. I wish I felt your head on my shoulder. I think I will go to bed.

I have been a half-hour writing this thing. Will you write something to me? I hope you will. How am I to sign myself? I won't sign anything at all, because I don't know what to sign myself.

Liszt, Franz
Famous Hungarian pianist, composer, conductor and teacher

Liszt, Franz

Franz Liszt (1811-1886), virtuoso pianist, composer, and piano teacher of the 19th century, took Paris by storm with his virtuoso performances. Of Hungarian descent, Liszt became renowned throughout Europe during the 19th century for his great skill as a performer. He was said by his contemporaries to have been the most technically advanced pianist of his age and perhaps the greatest pianist of all time.

It was during these years in Paris that Liszt met his future wife, the young and beautiful Countess D'Agoult. Unhappily married and in a separation, she fell madly in love with Liszt. Under her influence, Liszt's creative output exploded. In 1834 Liszt debuted as a mature and original composer with his piano compositions Harmonies poetiques et religieuses and the set of three Apparitions. These were all poetic works which contrasted strongly with the fantasies he had written earlier.
In 1835 the countess left her husband and family to join Liszt in Geneva; their daughter Blandine was born there on December 18. For the next four years Liszt and the countess lived together, mainly in Switzerland and Italy, where their daughter, Cosima, was born in Como, with occasional visits to Paris. On May 9, 1839 Liszt and the countess's only son, Daniel, was born, but that autumn relations between them became strained. The countess eventually returned to Paris with the children.

For the next eight years Liszt continued to tour Europe; spending holidays with the countess and their children on the island of Nonnenwerth on the Rhine in summers 1841 and 1843. In spring 1844 the couple finally separated.

Love Letters of Great Men

Thursday morning 1834

My heart overflows with emotion and joy! I do not know what heavenly languor, what infinite pleasure permeates it and burns me up. It is as if I had never loved!!! Tell me whence these uncanny disturbances spring, these inexpressible foretastes of delight, these divine, tremors of love. Oh! all this can only spring from you, sister, angel, woman, Marie! All this can only be, is surely nothing less than a gentle ray streaming from your fiery soul, or else some secret poignant teardrop which you have long since left in my breast.

My God, my God, never force us apart, take pity on us! But what am I saying? Forgive my weakness, how couldst Thou divide us! Thou wouldst have nothing but pity for us...No no! It is not in vain that our flesh and our souls quicken and become immortal through Thy Word, which cries out deep within us Father, Father...out Thy hand to us, that our broken hearts seek their refuge in Thee...O! we thank, bless and praise Thee, O God, for all that Thou has given us, and all that Thou hast prepared for us....

This is to be—to be! Marie! Marie!

Oh let me repeat that name a hundred times, a thousand times over; for three days now it has lived within me, oppressed me, set me afire. I am not writing to you, no, I am close beside you. I see you, I hear you. Eternity in your arms... Heaven, Hell, everything, all is within you, redoubled...Oh! Leave me free to rave in my delirium. Drab, tame, constricting reality is no longer enough for me. We must live our lives to the full, loving and suffering to extremes!...

Franz

London, Jack

American author, journalist, social activist

London, Jack

Jack London (1876–1916) was an American author who wrote The Call of the Wild, White Fang, and The Sea Wolf along with many other popular books. A pioneer in the then-burgeoning world of commercial magazine fiction, he was one of the first Americans to make a lucrative career exclusively from writing.

Though married to Bessie Maddern at the time, London continued a his friendship with Anna Strunsky, co-authoring The Kempton-Wace Letters, an epistolary novel contrasting two philosophies of love. Anna, writing "Dane Kempton's" letters, arguing for a romantic view of marriage, while London, writing "Herbert Wace's" letters, argued for a scientific view, based on Darwinism and eugenics.

Bessie and others mistakenly perceived Anna Strunsky as her rival, while another friend, Charmian Kittredge, mendaciously gave Bessie the impression of being sympathetic.

After divorcing Bessie, London married Charmian Kittredge, who was later called "Jack's soul-mate, always at his side, and a perfect match." The letter to the right was written by Jack London to Anna Strunsky, suggesting that a romance did exist between them at one time.

Dear Anna,

Did I say that the humans might be filed in categories? Well, and if I did, let me qualify—not all humans. You elude me. I cannot place you, cannot grasp you. I may boast that of nine out of ten, under given circumstances, I can forecast their action; that of nine out of ten, by their word or action, I may feel the pulse of their hearts. But of the tenth I despair. It is beyond me. You are that tenth.

Were ever two souls, with dumb lips, more incongruously matched! We may feel in common—surely, we oftimes do—and when we do not feel in common, yet do we understand; and yet we have no common tongue. Spoken words do not come to us. We are unintelligible. God must laugh at the mummery. The one gleam of sanity through it all is that we are both large temperamentally, large enough to often understand.

True, we often understand but in vague glimmering ways, by dim perceptions, like ghosts, which, while we doubt, haunt us with their truth. And still, I, for one, dare not believe; for you are that tenth which I may not forecast. Am I unintelligible now? I do not know. I imagine so. I cannot find the common tongue.

Large temperamentally—that is it. It is the one thing that brings us at all in touch. We have, flashed through us, you and I, each a bit of universal, and so we draw together. And yet we are so different.

I smile at you when you grow enthusiastic. It is a forgivable smile—nay, almost an envious smile. I have lived twenty-five years of repression. I learned not to be enthusiastic. It is a hard lesson to forget. I begin to forget, but it is so little. At the best, before I die, I cannot hope to forget all or most. I can exult, now that I am learning, in little things, in other things; but of my things, and secret things doubly mine, I cannot, I cannot. Do I make myself intelligible? Do you hear my voice? I fear not. There are poseurs. I am the most successful of them all.

Jack

Mozart, Wolfgang Amadeus

Prolific and influential composer of the classical era

Mozart, Wolfgang Amadeus

Wolfgang Amadeus Mozart (1756-91) was born in Salzburg, the son of Leopold Mozart and Anna Maria Pertl. As a child prodigy, he wowed the courts of Austria. From the age of five he performed all over Europe with his sister, Maria-Anna. As an adult, Mozart was a prolific and influential composer of the Classical era. He composed over 600 works, many acknowledged as pinnacles of symphonic, concertante, chamber, piano, operatic, and choral music. He is among the most enduringly popular of classical composers.

Mozart showed prodigious ability from his earliest childhood in Salzburg. Already competent on keyboard and violin, he composed from the age of five and performed before European royalty; at 17 he was engaged as a court musician in Salzburg, but grew restless and traveled in search of a better position, always composing abundantly.

Mozart learned voraciously from others, and developed a brilliance and maturity of style that encompassed the light and graceful along with the dark and passionate—the whole informed by a vision of humanity "redeemed through art, forgiven, and reconciled with nature and the absolute."

This is a portion of a long letter sent by Wolfgang Mozart to his wife Constanze from whom he was often separated. As a professional musician he would often have to visit cities in other countries to play for important people usually royalty or people with lots of money. This romantic postscript was added to a letter written only a year or so before he died of heart failure at the age of 35.

PS

While I was writing the last page, tear after tear fell on the paper. But I must cheer up—catch!—An astonishing number of kisses are flying about—The deuce!—I see a whole crowd of them! Ha! Ha!...I have just caught three—They are delicious! You can still answer this letter, but you must address your reply to Linz, Poste Restante - That is the safest course. As I do not yet know for certain whether I shall go to Regensburg, I can't tell you anything definite. Just write on the cover that the letter is to be kept until called for.

Adieu - Dearest, most beloved little wife—Take care of your health —and don't think of walking into town. Do write and tell me how you like our new quarters—Adieu. I kiss you millions of times.

Murry, John Middleton
Prolific English writer and prominent critic

Murry, John Middleton

John Middleton Murry (1889–1957) was an English writer. He was prolific, producing more than 60 books and thousands of essays and reviews on literature, social issues, politics, and religion during his lifetime. A prominent critic, Murry is best remembered for his association with Katherine Mansfield, whom he married as her second husband, in 1918. Following Mansfield's death, he edited her work.

Kathleen Mansfield Murry (1888–1923) was a prominent modernist writer of short fiction who was born and brought up in colonial New Zealand and wrote under the pen name of Katherine Mansfield. When Mansfield submitted a lightweight story to a new avant-garde magazine called Rhythm, the piece was rejected by the magazine's editor, John Middleton Murry, who requested something darker. Thus Mansfield and Murray began a relationship that would culminate in their marriage in 1918.

They led a troubled life during this time. In October 1912, the publisher of Rhythm, Stephen Swift, absconded to Europe, and left Murry responsible for the debts the magazine had accumulated. Mansfield and Murry moved to a village in Buckinghamshire in 1913, in an attempt to alleviate Mansfield of her ill health. Later that year, they moved to Paris, with the hope that the change of setting would make writing for both of them easier. At the beginning of 1917, Mansfield and Murry separated, although he continued to visit her at her new apartment. Mansfield's health continued to fail, and she died five years later, in 1923.

From Katherine Mansfield
To John Middleton Murry

Spring 1919

My love for you tonight is so deep and tender that it seems to be outside myself as well. I am fast shut up like a little lake in the embrace of some big mountains. If you were to climb up the mountains, you would see me down below, deep and shining - and quite fathomless, my dear. You might drop your heart into me and you'd never hear it touch bottom.

I love you—I love you—Goodnight.

Oh Bogey, what it is to love like this!

Peary, Robert

American explorer who claimed to have led the first
expedition to the North Pole

Peary, Robert

Robert Edwin Peary (1856–20, 1920) was an American explorer who claimed to have been the first person, on April 6, 1909, to reach the geographic North Pole. Peary's claim was widely credited for most of the 20th century, though it was criticized even in its own day and is today widely doubted.

Peary joined the navy at age 24, which gave him leave of absence for Arctic exploration. He made his first expedition to Greenland in 1886 with his lifelong associate Matthew Henson; on his second expedition in 1891 he discovered Independence Fjord and brought back evidence of Greenland being an island. Attempts to reach the North Pole in 1900, 1902, and 1905 all ended in failure. Finally, in 1909 he announced to the world that he had succeeded.

That same year his rival Dr. Fredrick Cook claimed to have reached the Pole a year earlier. Cook's claim was dismissed, and Peary's was eventually accepted, in spite of widespread doubt. He retired as a rear admiral in 1911, and lived with his family in Eagle Island off the coast of Maine until his death nine years later. Peary's wife, Josephine, accompanied him on several of his expeditions.

August 17, 1908
S.S. Roosevelt,
My Darling Josephine:

Am nearly through with my writing. Am brain weary with the thousand and one imperative details and things to think of.

Everything thus far has gone well, too well I am afraid, and I am (solely on general principles) somewhat suspicious of the future. The ship is in better shape than before; the party and crew are apparently harmonious; I have 21 Eskimo men (against 23 last time) but the total of men women and children is only 50 as against 67 before owing to a more careful selection as to children... I have landed supplies here, and leave two men ostensibly on behalf of Cook. As a matter of fact I have established here the sub-base which last I established at Victoria Head, as a precaution in event of loss of the Roosevelt either going up this fall or coming down next summer. In some respects this is an advantage as on leaving here there is nothing to delay me or keep me from taking either side of the Channel going up. the conditions give me entire control of the situation...

You have been with me constantly, sweetheart. At Kangerdlooksoah I looked repeatedly at Ptarmigan Island and thought of the time we camped there. At Nuuatoksoah I landed where we were. And on the 11th we passed the mouth of Bowdoin Bay in brilliant weather, and as long as I could I kept my eyes on Anniversary Lodge. We have been great chums dear. Tell Marie to remember what I told her, tell "Mister Man" [Robert Peary, Jr.] to remember "straight and strong and clean and honest", obey orders, and never forget that Daddy put

"Mut" in his charge till he himself comes back to take her. In fancy I kiss your dear eyes and lips and cheeks sweetheart; and dream of you and my children, and my home till I come again. Kiss my babies for me. Aufwiedersehen.

Love, Love, Love.
Your Bert

P.S. August 18, 9 a.m. ...Tell Marie that her fir pillow perfumes me to sleep.

Poe, Edgar Allan
American poet, author, and literary critic

Poe, Edgar Allan

Edgar Allan Poe (1809–1849) was an American writer, poet, editor and literary critic, considered part of the American Romantic Movement. Best known for his tales of mystery and the macabre, Poe was one of the earliest American practitioners of the short story and is considered the inventor of the detective-fiction genre. He is further credited with contributing to the emerging genre of science fiction. He was the first well-known American writer to try to earn a living through writing alone, resulting in a financially difficult life and career.

Early in his career as a writer, Poe spent several years working for literary journals and periodicals, becoming known for his style of literary criticism. His work forced him to move between several cities, including Baltimore, Philadelphia, and New York City. In Baltimore in 1835, he married Virginia Clemm, his 13-year-old cousin. Just seven years later, Virginia died of tuberculosis.

After the death of Virginia, Poe published his poem "The Raven" to instant success. Poe and his works influenced literature in the United States and around the world, as well as in specialized fields, such as cosmology and cryptography.

Increasingly unstable after his wife's death, Poe attempted to court the poet Sarah Helen Whitman, who lived in Providence, Rhode Island. Their engagement failed, purportedly because of Poe's drinking and erratic behavior. There is also strong evidence that Whitman's mother intervened and did much to derail their relationship.The letter to the right is one that Poe wrote to Sarah Whitman.

At or around October 1, 1848

I cannot better explain to you what I felt than by saying that your unknown heart seemed to pass into my bosom – there to dwell forever —while mine, I thought, was translated into your own.

From that hour I loved you. Yes, I now feel that it was then— on that evening of sweet dreams – that the very first dawn of human love burst upon the icy night of my spirit. Since that period I have never seen nor heard your name without a shiver half of delight, half of anxiety… for years your name never past my lips, while my soul drank in, with a delirious thirst, all that was uttered in my presence respecting you.

The merest whisper that concerned you awoke in me a shuddering sixth sense, vaguely compounded of fear, ecstatic happiness, and a wild, inexplicable sentiment that resembled nothing so nearly as the consciousness of guilt.

Raleigh, Sir Walter

English aristocrat, writer, poet, soldier, courtier, spy, and explorer who popularized tobacco in England

Raleigh, Sir Walter

Sir Walter Raleigh (1552-1618) was an English colonizer, courtier, historian and explorer. He was a favorite courtier of Queen Elizabeth I and was knighted by her in 1584.

In 1603 Raleigh was wrongly tried and convicted of treason against the crown, having been set up by one of his enemies in the royal court. His sentence was immediate death. Imprisoned in the Tower of London on what he believed was the eve of his execution, he composed a loving farewell to his wife, Elizabeth (not the queen).

He was not executed the following morning but remained confined in the Tower of London until 1616, when he was released to lead an expedition in search of gold for the crown. However, in 1618 he was returned to the Tower of London and executed by the harsh hand of Queen Elizabeth I's successor, James I.

1603

You shall now receive (my dear wife) my last words in these my last lines. My love I send you that you may keep it when I am dead, and my counsel that you may remember it when I am no more.

I would not by my will present you with sorrows (dear Besse) let them go to the grave with me and be buried in the dust. And seeing that it is not God's will that I should see you any more in this life, bear it patiently, and with a heart like thy self.

First, I send you all the thanks which my heart can conceive, or my words can rehearse for your many travails, and care taken for me, which though they have not taken effect as you wished, yet my debt to you is not the less; but pay it I never shall in this world.

Secondly, I beseech you for the love you bear me living, do not hide yourself many days, but by your travails seek to help your miserable fortunes and the right of your poor child. Thy mourning cannot avail me, I am but dust...

Remember your poor child for his father's sake, who chose you, and loved you in his happiest times. Get those letters which I wrote to the Lords, wherein I sued for my life; God is my witness it was for you and yours that I desired life, but it is true that I disdained myself for begging of it: for know it that your son is the son of a true man, and one who in his own respect despiseth death and all his misshapen and ugly forms.

I cannot write much, God he knows how hardly I steal this time while others sleep, and it is also time that I should separate my thoughts from the world. Beg my dead body which living was denied thee; and either lay it at Sherburne or in Exeter Church, by my Father and Mother; I can say no more, time and death call me away....

Written with the dying hand of sometimes thy Husband, but now alas overthrown.

Yours that was, but now not my own.

Walter Raleigh

Schumann, Robert
Influential German composer and music critic

Schumann, Robert

Robert Schumann, the seventeenth century German composer and pianist is known for his enduring operas and piano pieces.

He is one of the most famous and important Romantic composers of the 19th century. Schumann had hoped to pursue a career as a virtuoso pianist, having been assured by his teacher and future father-in-law, Friedrich Wieck, that he could become the finest pianist in Europe after only a few years of study with him. However, when a self-inflicted hand injury prevented those hopes from being realized, he decided to focus his musical energies on composition.

Schumann first fell in love with Clara Wieck during his early piano training under the instruction of Friederich Wieck. Clara herself was a virtuoso pianist and her father was bitterly opposed to the match. In his persistence, Robert went to court to seek legal consent for the marriage. The consent was obtained, and the couple was soon married.

In 1840, after a long and acrimonious legal battle with Wieck, Schumann married Clara, who also composed music and had a considerable concert career, including premieres of many of her husband's works.

Love Letters of Great Men

1838

Clara,

How happy your last letters have made me — those since Christmas Eve! I should like to call you by all the endearing epithets, and yet I can find no lovelier word than the simple word 'dear,' but there is a particular way of saying it. My dear one, then, I have wept for joy to think that you are mine, and often wonder if I deserve you.

One would think that no one man's heart and brain could stand all the things that are crowded into one day. Where do these thousands of thoughts, wishes, sorrows, joys and hopes come from? Day in, day out, the procession goes on. But how light-hearted I was yesterday and the day before! There shone out of your letters so noble a spirit, such faith, such a wealth of love!

What would I not do for love of you, my own Clara! The knights of old were better off; they could go through fire or slay dragons to win their ladies, but we of today have to content ourselves with more prosaic methods, such as smoking fewer cigars, and the like. After all, though, we can love, knights or no knights; and so, as ever, only the times change, not men's hearts...

You cannot think how your letter has raised and strengthened me... You are splendid, and I have much more reason to be proud of you than you of me. I have made up my mind, though, to read all your wishes in your face. Then you will think, even though you don't say it, that your Robert is a really good sort, that he is entirely yours, and he loves you more than words can say.

You shall indeed have cause to think so in the happy future. I still see you as you looked in your little cap that last evening. I still hear you call me du. Clara, I heard nothing of what you said but that du. Don't you remember?

But I see you in many another unforgettable guise. Once you were in a black dress, going to the theatre with Emilia List; it was during our separation. I know you will not have forgotten; it is vivid with me. Another time you were walking in the Thomasgasschen with an umbrella up, and you avoided me in desperation. And yet another time, as you were putting on your hat after a concert, our eyes happened to meet, and yours were full of the old unchanging love.

I picture you in all sorts of ways, as I have seen you since. I did not look at you much, but you charmed me so immeasurably... Ah, I can never praise you enough for yourself or for your love of me, which I don't really deserve.

Robert

Thomas, Dylan
Welsh poet and writer

Thomas, Dylan

Dylan Marlais Thomas (1914–1953) was a Welsh poet and writer who wrote exclusively in English. In addition to poetry, he wrote short stories and scripts for film and radio, which he often performed himself. His public readings, particularly in America, won him great acclaim; his sonorous voice with a subtle Welsh lilt became almost as famous as his works. His best-known works include the "play for voices" Under Milk Wood and the celebrated villanelle for his dying father, "Do not go gentle into that good night."

Thomas was famous for his personal readings, as Americans loved his lilting accent. In the spring of 1936, Dylan Thomas met Caitlin MacNamara, a dancer. They met in the Wheatsheaf public house, in the Fitzrovia area of London's West End. They were introduced by Augustus John, who was MacNamara's lover at the time (there were rumors that she continued her relationship with John after she married Thomas). A drunken Thomas proposed marriage on the spot, and the two began a courtship.

On July 11, 1937, Thomas married MacNamara at Penzance registry office in Cornwall. In 1938 the couple rented a cottage in the place Thomas was to help make famous, the village of Laugharne in Carmarthenshire, West Wales. Thomas wrote this letter to his Caitlin, who he affectionately called "Cat," when he was away from her, doing a book tour.

March 16, 1950

Cat: my cat: If only you would write to me: My love, oh Cat. This is not, as it seems from the address above, a dive, a joint, saloon, etc. but the honourable & dignified headquarters of the dons of the University of Chicago.

I love you. That is all I know. But all I know, too, is that I am writing into space: the kind of dreadful, unknown space I am just going to enter. I am going to Iowa, Illinois, Idaho, Indiana, but these, though misspelt, are on the map. You are not.

Have you forgotten me? I am the man you used to say you loved. I used to sleep in your arms—do you remember? But you never write. You are perhaps mindless of me. I am not of you. I love you.

There isn't a moment of any hideous day when I do not say to myself. 'It will be alright. I shall go home. Caitlin loves me. I love Caitlin.' But perhaps you have forgotten. If you have forgotten, or lost your affection for me, please, my Cat, let me know. I love you.

Dylan

Twain, Mark
American author and humorist

Twain, Mark

Mark Twain, who was born Samuel Langhorne Clemens (1835–1910), was an American author and humorist. Twain is noted for his novels Adventures of Huckleberry Finn, which has been called "the Great American Novel", and The Adventures of Tom Sawyer. He is extensively quoted. Twain was a friend to presidents, artists, industrialists, and European royalty.

Twain was very popular, and his keen wit and incisive satire earned praise from critics and peers. Upon his death he was lauded as the "greatest American humorist of his age", and William Faulkner called Twain "the father of American literature".

When Charles Langdon showed a picture of his sister, Olivia, to Twain, Twain claimed to have fallen in love at first sight. The two met in 1868, were engaged a year later, and married in February 1870 in Elmira, New York. Olivia came from a "wealthy but liberal family", and through her he met abolitionists, "socialists, principled atheists and activists for women's rights and social equality", including Harriet Beecher Stowe, Frederick Douglass, and the writer and utopian socialist William Dean Howells, who became a longtime friend.

This letter is from Mark Twain to Olivia, before they were married.

May 12, 1869

Out of the depths of my happy heart wells a great tide of love and prayer for this priceless treasure that is confided to my life-long keeping.

You cannot see its intangible waves as they flow towards you, darling, but in these lines you will hear, as it were, the distant beating of the surf.

Van Gogh, Vincent
Dutch post-Impressionist painter whose work, notable for its
rough beauty, emotional honesty, and bold color

Van Gogh, Vincent

Vincent van Gogh (1853–1890) was a Dutch post-Impressionist painter whose work had a far-reaching influence on 20th century art for its vivid colors and emotional impact.

Little appreciated during his lifetime, his fame grew in the years after his death. Today, he is widely regarded as one of history's greatest painters and an important contributor to the foundations of modern art. Van Gogh did not begin painting until his late twenties, and most of his best-known works were produced during his final two years. He produced more than 2,000 artworks, consisting of around 900 paintings and 1,100 drawings and sketches. Today many of his pieces—including his numerous self-portraits, landscapes, portraits and sunflowers—are among the world's most recognizable and expensive works of art.

Van Gogh spent his early adulthood working for a firm of art dealers and traveled between The Hague, London and Paris, after which he taught in England. An early vocational aspiration was to become a pastor and preach the gospel, and from 1879 he worked as a missionary in a mining region in Belgium. During this time he began to sketch people from the local community, and in 1885 painted his first major work The Potato Eaters.

His palette at the time consisted mainly of sombre earth tones and showed no sign of the vivid coloration that distinguished his later work. In March 1886, he moved to Paris and discovered the French Impressionists. Later he moved to the south of France and was taken by the strong sunlight he found there. His work grew brighter in color and he developed the unique and highly recognizable style which became fully realized during his stay in Arles in 1888.

Vincent Van Gogh is perhaps most famous for his yellow sunflower painting. He lived in Holland in the 1800s. He was desperately in love with his cousin, but his cousin refused to marry him. This letter was written by Vincent to his brother, Theo, talking about his love for his cousin.

September 7, 1881

Life has become very dear to me, and I am very glad that I love. My life and my love are one. "But you are faced with a 'no, never never'" is your reply. My answer to that is, "Old boy, for the present I look upon that 'no, never never' as a block of ice which I press to my heart to thaw."

Vincent Van Gogh

Voltaire
French Enlightenment writer, historian, and philosopher

Voltaire

François-Marie Arouet (1694–1778), better known by the pen name Voltaire, was a French Enlightenment writer and philosopher famous for his wit and for his advocacy of civil liberties, including freedom of religion and free trade.

Voltaire was a prolific writer and produced works in almost every literary form including plays, poetry, novels, essays, historical and scientific works, more than 20,000 letters and more than 2,000 books and pamphlets. He was an outspoken supporter of social reform, despite strict censorship laws and harsh penalties for those who broke them. As a satirical polemicist, he frequently made use of his works to criticize intolerance, [church] dogmas and the French institutions of his day.

Voltaire was one of several Enlightenment figures (along with Montesquieu, John Locke and Jean-Jacques Rousseau) whose works and ideas influenced important thinkers of both the American and French Revolutions.

At the age of nineteen Voltaire was sent as an attache to the French Ambassador to the Netherlands. It was there that he fell in love with Olympe Dunover, the poor daughter of a lower-class women. Their relationship was not approved of by either the ambassador of Olympe's mother and Voltaire was soon imprisoned to keep them apart. Voltaire wrote this passionate letter to his sweetheart while in prison. Shortly after, Voltaire managed to escape by climbing out of the window.

The Hague
1713

I am a prisoner here in the name of the King; they can take my life, but not the love that I feel for you.

Yes, my adorable mistress, to-night I shall see you, if I had to put my head on the block to do it.

For heaven's sake, do not speak to me in such disastrous terms as you write; you must live and be cautious; beware of Madame your mother as of your worst enemy.

What do I say?

Beware of everybody; trust no one; keep yourself in readiness, as soon as the moon is visible; I shall leave the hotel incognito, take a carriage or a chaise, we shall drive like the wind to Sheveningen; I shall take paper and ink with me; we shall write our letters.

If you love me, reassure yourself; and call all your strength and presence of mind to your aid; do not let your mother notice anything, try to have your pictures, and be assured that the menace of the greatest tortures will not prevent me to serve you.

No, nothing has the power to part me from you; our love is based upon virtue, and will last as long as our lives.

Adieu, there is nothing that I will not brave for your sake; you deserve much more than that.

Adieu, my dear heart!

Arout
(Voltaire)

Wilson, Woodrow
28th President of the United States

Wilson, Woodrow

Woodrow Wilson (1856–1924) was the 28th President of the United States. A leading intellectual of the Progressive Era, he served as President of Princeton University from 1902 to 1910, and then as the Governor of New Jersey from 1911 to 1913. With Theodore Roosevelt and William Howard Taft dividing the Republican Party vote, Wilson was elected President as a Democrat in 1912.

Woodrow Wilson was admired as a writer, a scholar, and an educator more than two decades before he became president. He spent twenty-four years working in the academic world as a professor, then as a college president, before he was elected governor of New Jersey. Two years later he was elected president of the United States, led the country through World War I (1914–18) and was the primary architect of the League of Nations.

This letter was written by President Woodrow Wilson to Edith Bolling Galt, who later became Edith Galt Wilson, Woodrow Wilson's second wife and First Lady of the United States.

The White House
September 19, 1915

My noble, incomparable Edith,

I do not know how to express or analyze the conflicting emotions that have surged like a storm through my heart all night long. I only know that first and foremost in all my thoughts has been the glorious confirmation you gave me last night - without effort, unconsciously, as of course - of all I have ever thought of your mind and heart.

You have the greatest soul, the noblest nature, the sweetest, most loving heart I have ever known, and my love, my reverence, my admiration for you, you have increased in one evening as I should have thought only a lifetime of intimate, loving association could have increased them.

You are more wonderful and lovely in my eyes than you ever were before; and my pride and joy and gratitude that you should love me with such a perfect love are beyond all expression, except in some great poem which I cannot write.

Your own,
Woodrow

18334774R00063

Made in the USA
Middletown, DE
07 March 2015